P9-DBY-929

SPIRIT OF '76
by A. M. Willard

from the original now at Abbot Hall, Marblehead, Mass.
"Also known as Yankee Doodle"

The
INAUGURAL
BOOK
1973

"The Spirit of '76"

Published by

1973 Inaugural Committee

First Edition

© 1973 by The 1973 Inaugural Committee. All rights reserved. No part of this book may be reproduced in any form, except by a reviewer, without the written permission of the 1973 Inaugural Committee or its duly appointed agent.
Library of Congress Catalog Card Number: 72-97727

Contents

On behalf of all of us in the official Government family, may I extend a warm welcome to each guest and participant in this Inaugural Week 1973.

This is the forty-seventh time in our history that Americans have gathered to solemnize and celebrate the orderly transfer or continuance of the Executive power in accord with the will of the people. Few events in our national life offer a grander spectacle of democracy in action or a more colorful portrait of the American people in moods both festive and thoughtful.

I hope that the activities of this inauguration will make it a joyous and memorable time for each of you—as it surely should be, considering the excellent preparations made under the leadership of Chairman Bill Marriott and the Inaugural Committee and outlined in this program book.

Most of all, I hope you will take home a new resolve to let the Spirit of '76 animate our American experience in the years ahead even more richly than it has before. In this, the Vice President and I and our colleagues in the Administration are pledged to do our utmost. We look forward to sharing with you in man's greatest adventure of all—freedom.

Richard Nixon

8

It is a privilege to be welcomed by you who have come to participate in this 47th Inauguration. I say "be welcomed" rather than "welcome," for truly the event belongs to the American people.

An inauguration is more than a ceremony, more than a program of activities and events. It is an infrequent, but consistently recurring moment in American life—dramatic, traditional, and symbolic of the people's control of this Republic. It is the vesting or re-vesting of executive power in a man, either to continue or change the course of the Nation. But for whatever purpose the people mandate, it is a regular, peaceful and orderly procedure. That is what makes it nearly unique in the world.

The oath which our President will take to preserve, protect and defend our Constitution remains the same oath which our first President, George Washington, swore nearly two centuries ago; and its historic words emphasize the importance of maintaining and building upon the foundations which were originally laid down for our system of government.

President Nixon and his Administration have served the American people for the last four years with those principles in mind. We have worked to bring about the reforms responsive to our changing times, while still conserving and working within our inherited framework of sound and tested values. America's enduring faith in these values has supported our endeavors and enabled us to continue the task we began four years ago.

Let us take the occasion of this Inaugural, combining tradition and the spirit of beginning anew, to rededicate ourselves to continuing progressive reform while preserving the principles which have made America a great Nation.

Spiro T. Agnew

J. Willard Marriott
Chairman
1973 Inaugural Committee

Jeb S. Magruder
Executive Director
1973 Inaugural Committee

A Presidential Inauguration is a celebration of democracy, a time when all Americans can take pride in the fact that we have devised a system of self-government which has worked for almost 200 years.

During President Nixon's second term, the United States will reach its 200th anniversary as an independent nation, and will celebrate the Fourth of July for the 200th time. Inaugural Day and Independence Day are somewhat similar. On both, we recognize the great American right of self-government and the privilege of voting for the candidates of our choice. On both days, we pause to remember that democracy is the greatest of our blessings—and we need only look to the nations which are deprived of it to appreciate fully what it means.

The President has chosen an appropriate theme for this Inauguration, "The Spirit of '76," to remind our nation to fully recapture the spirit of a Free America which was established by our forefathers in 1776.

The tremendous achievements of President Nixon during the past four years are so impressive that every American should feel fortunate in having the competent and dedicated leadership of this great man and his Vice President to manage our ship of state for another term.

I appreciate and thank the thousands of volunteers and committee members who have made our Inauguration events possible.

The Inaugural Week Schedule

Reception to Honor The Vice President and Mrs. Agnew

The Smithsonian Museum of History and Technology
By Special Invitation   5:00 p.m.–9:00 p.m.   Informal

A Salute to the States

The John F. Kennedy Memorial Center for the Performing Arts
By Special Invitation   9:00 p.m.   Informal

A Salute to America's Heritage

The Corcoran Gallery of Art
By Special Invitation   2:00 p.m.–6:00 p.m.   Informal

1973 Inaugural Concerts

The John F. Kennedy Memorial Center for the Performing Arts
All concerts by Special Invitation

Symphonic Concert—Concert Hall 9:00 p.m.		Black Tie Optional
Candlelight Dinner 6:00 p.m.		By Special Invitation
American Music Concert—Opera House 7:30 p.m.		Black Tie Optional
Candlelight Dinner—Following the concert		By Special Invitation
Youth Concert—Eisenhower Theatre 8:30 p.m.		Informal
		By Special Invitation

Official Inaugural Ceremony

East Portico, The Capitol   11:30 a.m.   By Special Invitation

Inaugural Parade

Pennsylvania Ave. (see map on page 15) 1:15 p.m.

Inaugural Balls

By Special Invitation   9:00 p.m.   Black Tie
Locations: The John F. Kennedy Memorial Center for the Performing Arts—The
Smithsonian Museum of History and Technology—The Smithsonian
Museum of Natural History—The Pension Building.
Inaugural Youth Ball   9:00 p.m.   Black Tie
Sheraton Park Hotel   By Special Invitation

White House Worship Service   11:30 a.m.   By Special Invitation

Special Inaugural Events

THURSDAY, JANUARY 18, 1973

A RECEPTION honoring The VICE PRESIDENT and MRS. AGNEW will be held at the Smithsonian Museum of History and Technology. This first Inaugural week event will take place from 5:00- 9:00 p.m. and is by special invitation only.

A SALUTE TO THE STATES will be held honoring the states and their governors starting at 9:00 p.m. This will be a two-and-one-half hour star-studded variety show featuring the top names in the performing arts. Inaugural guests will be entertained in the Opera House and the Concert Hall of the Kennedy Center (this event will replace the previously held Governor's Reception and the All American Gala). By special invitation only.

FRIDAY, JANUARY 19, 1973

A SALUTE TO AMERICA'S HERITAGE will be held honoring the contribution of America's ethnic and minority groups to American culture. The Corcoran Gallery of Art will be the scene of this festival from 2:00 p.m. to 6:00 p.m. featuring the music, art and food of a broad cross-section of America, presented in an informal and festive party manner similar to a neighborhood block party, with celebrity co-hosts. By special invitation only.

SUNDAY, JANUARY 21, 1973

A WORSHIP SERVICE in the East Room of the White House at 11:30 a.m. which will conclude the official Inaugural program of events. By special invitation only.

The Inaugural Concerts

FRIDAY, JANUARY 19, 1973

An evening of fine music has been a tradition of Presidential Inaugurals and 1973 will be no exception. For the first time, there will be three concerts which will take place in the three halls within the Kennedy Center.

SYMPHONIC CONCERT, at 9:00 p.m. in the Concert Hall, features Van Cliburn and the Philadelphia Symphony Orchestra under the direction of Eugene Ormandy. By special invitation only.

AMERICAN MUSIC CONCERT, at 7:30 p.m. in the Opera House, features half a dozen of the country's finest entertainers in concert format. By special invitation only.

YOUTH CONCERT, at 8:30 p.m. in the Eisenhower Theatre, presents music by top musicians whose primary appeal is to the young. By special invitation only.

CANDLELIGHT DINNERS FOR SPECIAL GUESTS of the INAUGURAL CONCERTS. The Roof Terrace of the Kennedy Center will be transformed into authentic 18th Century surroundings in keeping with the overall Colonial theme of the Candlelight Dinners. The total elegance of this period will be enhanced by a gourmet meal, appropriate decorations, hostesses in costumes and music of the period. By special invitation only.

Official Inaugural Ceremony

SATURDAY, JANUARY 20, 1973

East Portico, The Capitol   11:30 a.m.

Invocation
by Reverend Edward V. Hill

Selection
by the United States Marine Band

Prayer
by Rabbi Seymour Siegel

The Oath of Office will be administered to the Vice President
by the Chief Justice of the United States,
The Honorable Warren E. Burger

Prayer
by His Eminence Iakovos

Selection
by the Joint Service Academies Chorus

The Oath of Office will be administered to the President
by the Chief Justice of the United States,
The Honorable Warren E. Burger

Four ruffles and flourishes, "Hail to the Chief,"
and 21-gun salute

Inaugural Address
by the President of the United States

Benediction
by His Eminence Terence Cardinal Cooke

"The Star-Spangled Banner"
by Miss Ethel Ennis, the Joint Service Academies Chorus
and the United States Marine Band

Inaugural Parade

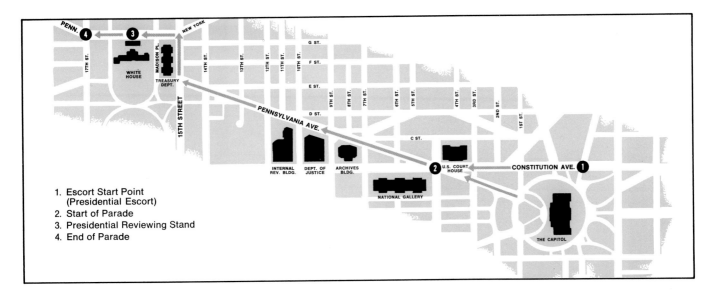

1. Escort Start Point
   (Presidential Escort)
2. Start of Parade
3. Presidential Reviewing Stand
4. End of Parade

SATURDAY, JANUARY 20, 1973

The Parade will last approximately one hour and forty-five minutes, starting at 1:15 p.m. on January 20th, representing America on the march, and reflecting the theme "The Spirit of '76."

The parade combines aspects of America's past, present, and future through flag displays, bands, horse units, marching units and floats. Each of the fifty states and territories is represented in the Parade.

Bands will be stationed along the parade route to entertain the crowds starting approximately 2 hours before the parade.

Inaugural Balls

SATURDAY, JANUARY 20, 1973

Beginning at 9:00 p.m., thousands of guests will celebrate the traditional climax to the Inaugural festivities, at the 1973 Inaugural Balls to be held at the John F. Kennedy Center for the Performing Arts and the Smithsonian's Museum of History and Technology, the Smithsonian Museum of Natural History and the Pension Building.

A new feature this year will be an Inaugural Youth Ball with music and decorations geared to the tastes of young people between the ages of 18 and 30, at the Sheraton Park Hotel.

"The Spirit of '76"

The Declaration of Independence by John Trumbull, Yale University Art Gallery

"The preservation of the sacred fire of liberty, and the destiny of the republican model of government, are ... staked on the experiment entrusted to the hands of the American people."

George Washington,
First Inaugural Address
April 30, 1789

It was Thomas Jefferson, in a letter to James Monroe, who first used the phrase "the Spirit of '76." For the new American nation, these words quickly came to represent the array of ideals and emotions which had surrounded its founding. Today "the Spirit of '76" still evokes those qualities which built America and which, for two centuries, have enabled it to preserve its greatness.

As the Nation approaches its 200th anniversary, "the Spirit of '76" takes on a double meaning. It points to the future as well as the past. It speaks not only of where we have been, but also of where we are going. It reminds us not only of our accomplishments but also of our objectives.

Because the Nation's bicentennial anniversary will be celebrated during the forthcoming Presidential administration, the 1973 inauguration has taken for its theme: "The Spirit of '76." This Inauguration provides an opportunity for all Americans to reflect again on the meaning of that spirit.

What is the "Spirit of '76"? Perhaps it is best expressed in the words of those who first helped to shape it.

"The God who gave us life, gave us liberty at the same time."

Thomas Jefferson,
*Summary View of the Rights
of British America, 1774*

"We hold these truths to be self-evident, that all men are created equal, that they are endowed by their Creator with certain unalienable rights, that among these are life, liberty, and the pursuit of happiness."

"And for the support of this declaration, with a firm reliance on the protection of Divine Providence, we mutually pledge to each other our lives, our fortunes, and our sacred honor."

Declaration of Independence

Old South Meeting House, Boston

"There, I guess King George will be able to read that."

John Hancock,
upon signing the Declaration
of Independence, July 4, 1776

18

*"Proclaim liberty
throughout the land
unto all
the inhabitants thereof."*

Leviticus, 25:10;
Inscription on
the Liberty Bell.

*"These are the times that try
men's souls. The summer
soldier and the sunshine
patriot will, in this crisis,
shrink from the service of his
country; but he that stands
it now deserves the love and
thanks of man and woman."*

Tom Paine: *The American Crisis*
No. 1, Dec. 23, 1776

"We are all Republicans—we are all Federalists. If there be any among us who would wish to dissolve this Union or to change its republican form, let them stand undisturbed as monuments of the safety with which error of opinion may be tolerated where reason is left free to combat it."

Thomas Jefferson,
First Inaugural Address
March 4, 1801

"You will think me transported with enthusiasm, but I am not. I am well aware of the toil, and blood, and treasure, that it will cost us to maintain this declaration, and support and defend these States. Yet, through all the gloom, I can see the rays of ravishing light and glory. I can see that the end is more than worth all the means, and that posterity will triumph in that day's transaction, even although we should rue it, which I trust in God we shall not. . . . The second day of July 1776, will be the most memorable epoch in the history of America. I am apt to believe that it will be celebrated by succeeding generations as the great anniversary festival. It ought to be commemorated as the day of deliverance, by solemn acts of devotion to God Almighty. It ought to be solemnized with pomp and parade, with shows, games, sports, guns, bells, bonfires, and illuminations, from one end of this continent to the other, from this time forward forevermore."

John Adams,
Letter to Mrs. Adams,
July 3, 1776

"*There is a time to pray and a time to fight. This is the time to fight.*"

John Peter Muhlenberg,
sermon, 1775

Preparing fortifications prior to battle of Bunker Hill, June 16, 1775

"*Let us contemplate our forefathers, and posterity, and resolve to maintain the rights bequeathed to us from the former, for the sake of the latter. The necessity of the times, more than ever, calls for our utmost circumspection, deliberation, fortitude and perseverance. Let us remember that 'if we suffer tamely a lawless attack upon our liberty, we encourage it, and involve others in our doom.' It is a very serious consideration . . . that millions yet unborn may be the miserable sharers in the event.*"

Samuel Adams,
Speech, 1771

"*I only regret that I have but one life to lose for my country.*"

Nathan Hale,
last words before being hanged
as a spy by the British,
New York, Sept. 22, 1776

"Ever since I arrived at the state of manhood, and acquainted myself with the general history of mankind, I have felt a sincere passion for liberty. The history of nations, doomed to perpetual slavery in consequence of yielding up to tyrants their natural-born liberties, I read with a sort of philosophical horror; so that the first systematical and bloody attempt, at Lexington, to enslave America thoroughly electrified my mind, and fully determined me to take part with my country."

Ethan Allen,
Narrative of his captivity, 1779

Gen. George Washington crossing the Delaware, Dec. 8, 1776

"The time is now near at hand which must probably determine whether Americans are to be freemen or slaves; whether they are to have any property they can call their own; whether their houses and farms are to be pillaged and destroyed, and themselves consigned to a state of wretchedness from which no human efforts will deliver them. The fate of unborn millions will now depend, under God, on the courage and conduct of this army. Our cruel and unrelenting enemy leaves us only the choice of a brave resistance, or the most abject submission. We have, therefore, to resolve to conquer or to die."

George Washington,
Address to American troops before the
Battle of Long Island, July, 1776

"Men, you are all marksmen—
don't one of you
fire until you see
the whites of their eyes."

Israel Putnam,
Battle of Bunker Hill,
June 17, 1775

"Don't give up the ship!
You will beat them off!"

James Mugford,
Boston Harbor,
May 19, 1776

"Don't Tread on Me."

Motto of first flag of
the Revolution, raised on
John Paul Jones's ship,
the *Alfred*, 1776

"I have not yet begun to fight!"

John Paul Jones,
Sept. 23, 1779

"I believe there are more
instances of the
abridgement of the
freedom of the people by
gradual and silent
encroachments of those in
power than by violent
and sudden usurpations."

James Madison,
Virginia Convention,
June 16, 1788

"Yet I will not believe our labors are lost. I shall not die without a hope that light and liberty are on steady advance . . . . the flames kindled on the 4th of July, 1776, have spread over too much of the globe to be extinguished by the feeble engines of despotism; on the contrary, they will consume these engines and all who work them."

Thomas Jefferson,
Letter to John Adams,
Monticello, Sept. 12, 1821

"They that can give essential liberty to obtain a little temporary safety deserve neither liberty nor safety."

Benjamin Franklin,
*Historical Review
of Pennsylvania*

FOURTH OF JULY CELEBRATION IN CENTER SQUARE, PHILADELPHIA, 1819
by John Lewis Krimmel

Library of Congress

". . . something in that declaration . . . gave promise that in due time the weights should be lifted from the shoulders of all men, and that all should have an equal chance."

Abraham Lincoln,
Address in Independence Hall,
February 22, 1861

"I must study politics and war, that my sons may have liberty to study mathematics and philosophy, geography, natural history and naval architecture, navigation, commerce, and agriculture, in order to give their children a right to study painting, poetry, music, architecture, statuary, tapestry, and porcelain."

John Adams

"There is nothing more common, than to confound the terms of the American revolution with those of the late American war. The American war is over: but this is far from being the case with the American revolution. On the contrary, nothing but the first act of the great drama is closed. It remains yet to establish and perfect our new forms of government; and to prepare the principles, morals, and manners of our citizens, for these forms of government, after they are established and brought to perfection."

Benjamin Rush,
"Address to the People of
the United States," 1787

Name	Born	Birthplace	Served	Age on Taking Off
1. George Washington	Feb. 22, 1732	Westmoreland County, Va.	1789-1797	57
2. John Adams	Oct. 30, 1735	Braintree, Mass.	1797-1801	61
3. Thomas Jefferson	Apr. 13, 1743	Albemarle County, Va.	1801-1809	57
4. James Madison	Mar. 16, 1751	Port Conway, Va.	1809-1817	57
5. James Monroe	Apr. 28, 1758	Westmoreland County, Va.	1817-1825	58
6. John Quincy Adams	July 11, 1767	Braintree, Mass.	1825-1829	57
7. Andrew Jackson	Mar. 15, 1767	Waxhaw, S. C.	1829-1837	61
8. Martin Van Buren	Dec. 5, 1782	Kinderhook, N. Y.	1837-1841	54
9. William H. Harrison	Feb. 9, 1773	Berkeley, Va.	1841	68
10. John Tyler	Mar. 29, 1790	Greenway, Va.	1841-1845	51
11. James K. Polk	Nov. 2, 1795	Pineville, N. C.	1845-1849	49
12. Zachary Taylor	Nov. 24, 1784	Orange County, Va.	1849-1850	64
13. Millard Fillmore	Jan. 7, 1800	Locke, N. Y.	1850-1853	50
14. Franklin Pierce	Nov. 23, 1804	Hillsboro, N. H.	1853-1857	48
15. James Buchanan	Apr. 23, 1791	Mercersburg, Pa.	1857-1861	65
16. Abraham Lincoln	Feb. 12, 1809	Hardin County, Ky.	1861-1865	52
17. Andrew Johnson	Dec. 29, 1808	Raleigh, N. C.	1865-1869	56
18. Ulysses S. Grant	Apr. 27, 1822	Point Pleasant, O.	1869-1877	46
19. Rutherford B. Hayes	Oct. 4, 1822	Delaware, O.	1877-1881	54
20. James A. Garfield	Nov. 19, 1831	Orange, O.	1881	49
21. Chester A. Arthur	Oct. 5, 1830	Fairfield, Vt.	1881-1885	50
22. Grover Cleveland	Mar. 18, 1837	Caldwell, N. J.	1885-1889	47
23. Benjamin Harrison	Aug. 20, 1833	North Bend, O.	1889-1893	55
24. Grover Cleveland	Mar. 18, 1837	Caldwell, N. J.	1893-1897	55
25. William McKinley	Jan. 29, 1843	Niles, O.	1897-1901	54
26. Theodore Roosevelt	Oct. 27, 1858	New York City	1901-1909	42
27. William H. Taft	Sept. 15, 1857	Cincinnati, O.	1909-1913	51
28. Woodrow Wilson	Dec. 28, 1856	Staunton, Va.	1913-1921	56
29. Warren G. Harding	Nov. 2, 1865	Morrow County, O.	1921-1923	55
30. Calvin Coolidge	July 4, 1872	Plymouth Notch, Vt.	1923-1929	51
31. Herbert Hoover	Aug. 10, 1874	West Branch, Ia.	1929-1933	54
32. Franklin D. Roosevelt	Jan. 30, 1882	Hyde Park, N. Y.	1933-1945	51
33. Harry S Truman	May 8, 1884	Lamar, Mo.	1945-1953	60
34. Dwight D. Eisenhower	Oct. 14, 1890	Denison, Tex.	1953-1961	62
35. John F. Kennedy	May 29, 1917	Brookline, Mass.	1961-1963	43
36. Lyndon B. Johnson	Aug. 27, 1908	Gillespie County, Tex.	1963-1969	55
37. Richard Nixon	Jan. 9, 1913	Yorba Linda, Calif.	1969-	56

Party	Died	Age at Death	Burial Place	Vice-President
Federalist	Dec. 14, 1799	67	Mount Vernon, Va.	John Adams
Federalist	July 4, 1826	90	Quincy, Mass.	Thomas Jefferson
Democratic-Republican	July 4, 1826	83	Monticello, Va.	Aaron Burr George Clinton
Democratic-Republican	June 28, 1836	85	Montpelier, Va.	George Clinton Elbridge Gerry
Democratic-Republican	July 4, 1831	73	Richmond, Va.	Daniel D. Tompkins
Democratic-Republican	Feb. 23, 1848	80	Quincy, Mass.	John C. Calhoun
Democratic	June 8, 1845	78	Hermitage, Tenn.	John C. Calhoun Martin Van Buren
Democratic	July 24, 1862	79	Kinderhook, N. Y.	Richard M. Johnson
Whig	Apr. 4, 1841	68	North Bend, O.	John Tyler
Whig	Jan. 18, 1862	71	Richmond, Va.	
Democratic	June 15, 1849	53	Nashville, Tenn.	George M. Dallas
Whig	July 9, 1850	65	Louisville, Ky.	Millard Fillmore
Whig	Mar. 8, 1874	74	Buffalo, N. Y.	
Democratic	Oct. 8, 1869	64	Concord, N. H.	William R. King
Democratic	June 1, 1868	77	Lancaster, Pa.	John C. Breckinridge
Republican	Apr. 15, 1865	56	Springfield, Ill.	Hannibal Hamlin Andrew Johnson
Democratic	July 31, 1875	66	Greeneville, Tenn.	
Republican	July 23, 1885	63	New York City	Schuyler Colfax Henry Wilson
Republican	Jan. 17, 1893	70	Fremont, O.	William A. Wheeler
Republican	Sept. 19, 1881	49	Cleveland, O.	Chester A. Arthur
Republican	Nov. 18, 1886	56	Albany, N. Y.	
Democratic	June 24, 1908	71	Princeton, N. J.	Thomas A. Hendricks
Republican	Mar. 13, 1901	67	Indianapolis, Ind.	Levi P. Morton
Democratic	June 24, 1908	71	Princeton, N. J.	Adlai E. Stevenson
Republican	Sept. 14, 1901	58	Canton, O.	Garret A. Hobart Theodore Roosevelt
Republican	Jan. 6, 1919	60	Oyster Bay, N. Y.	Charles W. Fairbanks
Republican	Mar. 8, 1930	72	Arlington, Va.	James S. Sherman
Democratic	Feb. 3, 1924	67	Washington, D.C.	Thomas R. Marshall
Republican	Aug. 2, 1923	57	Marion, O.	Calvin Coolidge
Republican	Jan. 5, 1933	60	Plymouth, Vt.	Charles G. Dawes
Republican	Oct. 20, 1964	90	West Branch, Ia.	Charles Curtis
Democratic	Apr. 12, 1945	63	Hyde Park, N. Y.	John N. Garner Henry A. Wallace Harry S Truman
Democratic	Dec. 26, 1972	88	Independence, Mo.	Alben W. Barkley
Republican	Mar. 28, 1969	78	Abilene, Kan.	Richard Nixon
Democratic	Nov. 22, 1963	46	Arlington, Va.	Lyndon B. Johnson
Democratic				Hubert H. Humphrey
Republican				Spiro Agnew

THE NIXON YEARS

...Forging A New Spirit of '76

"Eight years from now, America will celebrate its 200th anniversary as a nation. ... What kind of nation we will be, what kind of a world we will live in, whether we shape the future in the image of our hopes, is ours to determine by our actions and our choices."

First Inaugural Address
January 20, 1969

It is difficult amid the jostle of politics and the relentless daily pressures of governing a great nation to think or act according to perspectives much longer than this year and next. But Richard Nixon is perhaps set apart among American leaders by the sweeping spans of history in which he sees himself and his country moving.

He bids for peace not only in our own time but for a generation and more; he summons the Nation to reform that will protect self-government for a century hence. The long view also seems to come naturally to this President as he looks back. For it is under his leadership that the significance of our approaching bicentennial has come to life for Americans—two centuries of expanding democracy, two centuries of quickening adventure, two centuries of rich, shared experience as one American people, all to culminate in 1976.

The Spirit of '76 was much in the new President's mind as he gave his First Inaugural Address in front of the Capitol on a biting cold Monday afternoon, January 20, 1969. "Eight years from now," he said, "America will celebrate its 200th anniversary as a nation. . . . What kind of nation we will be, what kind of a world we will live in, whether we shape the future in the image of our hopes, is ours to determine by our actions and our choices."

Half of those eight years—half of what history will call the Nixon years—are behind us now. In that time the President and the people together have set in motion great enterprises aimed at ensuring that when 1976 comes we will be a nation whose goodness and greatness are at their zenith, living in a world where all mankind is at peace. Last fall, resoundingly, the voters chose Richard Nixon and Spiro Agnew to continue from these beginnings and to build on these achievements during the coming Presidential term.

Scanning the past four years and the next four

as that term begins, Americans can feel the Spirit of 1776 and of 1976 still shaping the "course of human events," still asserting the inalienable rights of all men to "life, liberty, and the pursuit of happiness," and reaffirming that "firm reliance on the protection of divine providence" which patriots from the signers of the Declaration of Independence to the men whose footprints now mark the moon have made their ultimate trust.

While we cannot know what the future holds, we do know that the American dream has come true over and over again in the two centuries past, and we can dare to shape still larger dreams for tomorrow.

The words of prophets at our Nation's birth have never seemed more alive than today in her maturity. For now more than ever before, we have the chance to prove that at home, as Tom Paine put it, "not a place on earth might be so happy as America"—and that around the world this country does act, in Jefferson's phrase, "not for ourselves alone, but for the whole human race."

THE FIRST TERM:

"I see our nation at peace in a world at peace"

Early in 1969, President Nixon set to work bringing to pass that shining vision which candidate Nixon had evoked with the "I see a day" litany in his speech accepting the Republican nomination the summer before. At the convention in Miami he had been speaking of a distant tomorrow in 1976; but at the inauguration ceremony in Washington, moments after the transfer of power, he talked more decisively of today: "The times are on the side of peace," he said of the international outlook; and of the troubled domestic scene: "We can build a great cathedral of the spirit."

He took office determined that his Presidency should make an important difference in America's quest for peace and justice—and convinced that the way to make a difference was to change the country's basic approach to foreign and domestic challenges.

In foreign affairs, the President instituted a comprehensive new policy which placed much greater emphasis on negotiation rather than confrontation with our adversaries, and on sharing responsibilities with our friends.

The success of this new approach was evidenced in many ways. America's ground combat role was ended in Vietnam. Over half a million men were withdrawn and a negotiated settlement pushed forward. The President's trips to the Soviet Union and the People's Republic of China symbolized our new relationships with those countries. Significant progress was achieved toward the all-important goal of arms control. A new agreement concerning Berlin, a ceasefire which has lasted for more than two years in the Middle East, and a new approach to foreign aid also testified to the President's success, as did his substantial progress toward new international systems of monetary exchange and trade.

These and other achievements mean that the chances to build a lasting structure of peace in the world are better now than at any time in the past generation.

The Nixon Administration has also been able to pare down the defense budget so that it now consumes a lower percentage of the Gross National Product than any since before the Korean War. For the first time in two decades, spending priorities now favor human resources rather than defense programs. Draft calls have been drastically reduced and the groundwork laid for ending the draft.

"*What we seek is not a Pax Americana,
not an American Century, but rather
a structure of stability and progress that
will enable each nation, large and small,
to chart its own course, to make its
own way without outside interference,
without intimidation, without domination
by ourselves or any other nation. . . .
Above all, let us, as leaders of the world,
reflect in our actions what our own people
feel. Let us do what our own people need.
Let us consider the world interest—
the people's interest—in all that we do.*"

Address to the U.N. General Assembly
October 23, 1970

MAJOR FOREIGN TRIPS OF PRESIDENT NIXON'S FIRST TERM

February-March 1969

Belgium   Italy
Great Britain   France
West Germany   The Vatican

July-August 1969

Around the world:
South Pacific—welcomes Apollo 11 astronauts home from the moon
Guam—enunciates Nixon Doctrine
Philippines
Indonesia
Thailand
South Vietnam
India
Pakistan
Romania
Great Britain

August 1970

Mexico

September-October 1970

Italy
Yugoslavia
Spain
Great Britain
Ireland

February 1972

People's Republic of China

April 1972

Canada

May-June 1972

Austria
Soviet Union
Iran
Poland

"When there is trust between men who are leaders of nations, there is a better chance to settle differences than when there is not trust. I think that one of the accomplishments of this trip is that we have established between the United States of America and the major nations of Europe . . . a new relationship of trust and confidence that did not exist before."

News conference after
return from Europe
March 4, 1969

"On my schedule it said: 'President Nixon will speak for 10 minutes and then his speech will be translated into English.' I knew I had troubles in communicating, but not that much."

Remarks to the
U.S. Embassy staff,
Paris, March 2, 1969

"I believe that the time has come when the United States,
in our relations with all of our Asian friends, (must) be quite
emphatic on two points: One, that we will keep
our treaty commitments . . . but, two, that as far as the
problems of internal security are concerned . . .
this problem will be increasingly handled by
. . . the Asian nations themselves."

The President outlining
the Nixon Doctrine
at Guam, July 25, 1969

". . . out here in this dreary, difficult war, I
think history will record that this may
have been one of America's finest hours,
because we took a difficult task and we
succeeded. You are doing your job. I can
assure you we are going to try to do ours
to see that you didn't fight in vain."

Remarks to U.S. troops
in Vietnam, July 30, 1969

"I am confident we will negotiate the
settlement which will end the war and
bring us what we all want—peace with
honor and not peace with surrender for
the United States of America."

Campaign speech, Ontario, California
November 4, 1972

THE PRESIDENT'S VISIT TO THE PEOPLE'S REPUBLIC OF CHINA

July 15, 1971   The President announces the invitation to visit Peking: "I will undertake . . . a journey for peace."

February 21, 1972   The President and Mrs. Nixon arrive in Peking and are greeted by Premier Chou En-lai; the President meets with Chairman Mao Tse-tung; U.S. party attends welcoming banquet.

February 22   Conferences with Premier Chou; Nixons attend ballet.

February 23   Conferences; Nixons attend sports show.

February 24   Conferences; visit to Great Wall and Ming Tombs.

February 25   Visit to Peking's Forbidden City; President's dinner for Chinese officials.

February 26   Final conferences; President and party fly to Hangchow.

February 27   President and party fly to Shanghai; official communiqué on the talks is issued.

February 28   The President arrives home in Washington.

"Let all nations know that during this administration our lines of communication will be open. We seek an open world—open to ideas, open to the exchange of goods and people—a world in which no people, great or small, will live in angry isolation."

First Inaugural Address
January 20, 1969

© UPI Compix

"We have demonstrated that nations with very deep and fundamental differences can learn to discuss those differences calmly, rationally, and frankly, without compromising their principles. This is the basis of a structure of peace, where we can talk about differences rather than fight about them."

Remarks upon return to
Washington from the Peking summit
February 28, 1972

STATE VISIT OF THE PRESIDENT TO THE SOVIET UNION

May 22, 1972
The President and Mrs. Nixon arrive in Moscow; first meeting with General Secretary Brezhnev; welcoming dinner in Kremlin Palace.

May 23
Signing of agreements on cooperation in health research and environmental protection.

May 24
Signing of agreements on joint space exploration and on cooperation in science.

May 25
Signing of agreement to prevent incidents at sea; Nixons attend "Swan Lake" at the Bolshoi Theater.

May 26
Signing of unprecedented agreement to begin checking the nuclear arms race by limiting offensive and defensive strategic weapons; establishment of commercial commission which completed comprehensive trade agreement later in 1972.

May 27
Sightseeing visit to Leningrad.

May 28
The President addresses the Soviet people on national television.

May 29
Signing of declaration of basic principles of U.S.-Soviet relations; U.S. party departs for Kiev.

June 1
The President returns to Washington following state visits to Iran and Poland en route home; reports on the Moscow summit before a Joint Session of the Congress: "The foundation has been laid for a new relationship between the two most powerful nations in the world."

"Those who would be our adversaries, we invite to a peaceful competition . . . in enriching the life of man. As we explore the reaches of space, let us go to the new worlds together . . . . With those who are willing to join, let us cooperate to reduce the burden of arms, to strengthen the structure of peace, to lift up the poor and the hungry."

First Inaugural Address
January 20, 1969

"*As great powers, we shall sometimes be competitors,
but we need never be enemies. . . . In many ways, the
people of our two countries are very much alike. . . .
We want for you and for your children the same peace and
abundance that we want for ourselves and for our children.*"

Address to the Soviet People
May 28, 1972

"We shall plan now for the day when our wealth can be transferred from the destruction of war abroad to the urgent needs of our people at home."

First Inaugural Address
January 1969

ON THE DOMESTIC SCENE, President Nixon inherited a wide range of complex problems accumulated during the turbulent decade of the 1960's. And he was the first President in more than a century to take office with both Houses of the Congress under opposition control. He has approached the assignment by making "reform" his watchword, by trusting the government less and the people more—and he has achieved significant results.

His new economic policy has guided the U.S. economy—for the first time since the Eisenhower years—into the first stages of a new prosperity, one which is not accompanied by inflation and not dependent on war. The job market has mushroomed, trade has increased, and taxes have been lowered.

With the initiation of the President's revenue sharing program, the historic flow of power to Washington has been reversed—making possible a new balance and a new vitality for the Federal system. Sweeping reorganization of the Federal Government has also been a central part of what the President has called "a new American revolution."

Reform was the hallmark of the President's proposals concerning the welfare system, the war against crime and drug abuse, the rebuilding of the cities, the development of rural areas, and the protection of the environment. Health, nutrition, transportation, education, housing and consumer protection are other programs which have moved forward during the first four Nixon years.

President Nixon also pressed forward with Federal efforts to achieve greater justice and opportunity for groups which have not always had the chance to share fully in the American experience. "Those who have been left out, we will try to bring in. Those left behind, we will help to catch up," said the President in his Inaugural Address—and that is precisely what he has done.

Perhaps the greatest crisis the new President faced as he delivered his First Inaugural Address in January of 1969 was what he called "a crisis of the spirit." And perhaps his greatest accomplishment has been helping the Nation find "an answer of the spirit" within itself.

In the past four years, a new sense of calm and confidence has begun to grow in America. A nation that had grown skeptical has been learning to trust its institutions again. A nation that had fallen into shouting and posturing has started to lower its voices. A nation that had become divided has begun to pull itself back together.

And because of the accomplishments of these four years, the American people could be confident as they looked to the next four, and to the Nation's approaching bicentennial, that the great experiment which began 200 years ago was moving forward once again.

"*If we are to stop the rise in the cost of living which is putting such a strain on the family budgets of millions of Americans, we have to cut the Federal budget. . . . no matter how popular a spending program is, if I determine that its enactment will have the effect of raising your prices or raising your taxes, I will not approve that program.*"

Address to the Nation
January 26, 1970

"*Prosperity without war requires action on three fronts: We must create more and better jobs; we must stop the rise in the cost of living; we must protect the dollar from the attacks of international money speculators. We are going to take that action—not timidly, not half-heartedly, not in piecemeal fashion. We are going to move forward to the new prosperity without war as befits a great people—all together, and along a broad front.*"

Address to the Nation
announcing the New Economic Policy
August 15, 1971

"*We are encouraged by the record of our current economic performance. We are now experiencing one of the lowest rates of inflation, one of the highest rates of real economic growth, of any industrial nation. Recent gains in the productivity and the real income of American workers have been heartening. We intend to continue the policies that have produced those gains.*"

Address to the International Monetary Fund
September 25, 1972

"We see the hope of tomorrow in the youth of today.
I know America's youth. I believe in them. We can be
proud that they are better educated, more committed,
more passionately driven by conscience than any generation
in our history."

First Inaugural Address
January 20, 1969

". . . what this Congress can be remembered for is
opening the way to a new American revolution—a peaceful
revolution in which power was turned back to the people—
in which government at all levels was refreshed and
renewed, and made truly responsive. This . . . can
mean that just 5 years from now America will enter its
third century as a young nation new in spirit, with all the
vigor and the freshness with which it began its first century."

State of the Union Message
January 22, 1971

"The Constitution of the United States begins with the
words 'We, the people,' and the bill I shall sign is a
demonstration of a principle that we have faith in people,
we believe in people, and we believe that government
closest to the people should have the greatest support."

Remarks upon signing the revenue sharing act,
Independence Hall, Philadelphia, October 20, 1972

"... we have fought the frightening trend of crime and anarchy to a standstill. ... We have moved off the defensive and onto the offensive in our all-out battle against the criminal forces in America. We are going to stay on the offensive until we put every category of crime on a downward trend in every American community."

Radio address
October 15, 1972

"Except for the contribution he may be able to make to the cause of world peace, there is probably no more important legacy that a President of the United States can leave in these times than his appointments to the Supreme Court . . . I believe that Chief Justice Burger, Mr. Justice Blackmun, by their conduct and their decisions, have earned the respect not only of those who supported them when I nominated them, but also those who opposed them. It is my firm conviction tonight that Lewis Powell and William Rehnquist will earn the same respect . . . as guardians of our Constitution."

The President discussing his Supreme Court appointees in a speech to the Nation, October 21, 1971

© 1973 NATIONAL GEOGRAPHIC SOCIETY Photo by Robert S. Oakes

"The 1970's absolutely must be the years when America pays its debt to the past by reclaiming the purity of its air, its waters, and our living environment. It is literally now or never . . . . We are determined that the decade of the seventies will be known as the time when this country regained a productive harmony between man and nature."

Statement by the President
January 1, 1970

"I wish it were possible to present a peace prize to every farmer and every farm family in America, in recognition of what they have done in years past to help keep our country strong and free, and in recognition also of what they can do in years ahead to help unite all peoples in a new alliance against the common enemies of mankind—hunger and poverty and misery in the world."

Radio address
October 27, 1972

". . . we must develop a new attitude toward aging in America, one that stops regarding older Americans as a burden and starts regarding them as a resource."

Radio address
October 30, 1972

". . . we are approaching the limits of what government alone can do. Our greatest need now is to reach beyond government, to enlist the legions of the concerned and the committed . . . . To match the magnitude of our tasks, we need the energies of our people . . . with these, we can build a great cathedral of the spirit."

———

"No man can be fully free while his neighbor is not. To go forward at all is to go forward together. . . . The laws have caught up with our conscience. What remains is to give life to what is in the law: to insure at last that as all are born equal in dignity before God, all are born equal in dignity before man."

First Inaugural Address
January 20, 1969

"*If we do not find a way to become a working nation that properly cares for the dependent, we shall become a Welfare State that undermines the incentive of the working man. . . . We have it in our power to raise the standard of living and the realizable hopes of millions of our fellow citizens. By providing an equal chance at the starting line, we can reinforce the traditional American spirit of self-reliance and self-respect.*"

Message to the Congress
proposing welfare reform
August 11, 1969

"A large vision of America has been put forth. It can only be furthered by men who share it. . . . I am of those who believe that America is the hope of the world, and that for that time given him the President is the hope of America. Serve him well. Pray for his success. Understand how much depends on you. Try to understand what he has given of himself."

Daniel P. Moynihan
Farewell remarks to the Cabinet
December 21, 1970

"Sometimes when I wake up in the middle of the night, half awake, and I think of the serious problems of this Nation and the world, I say to myself, 'I have got to talk to the President about that problem.' And then when I am fully awake, I realize that I am the President."

Remarks to students from
the North American College, The Vatican,
September 28, 1970

"I want to be quite candid with regard to the relationship of the President with the House of Representatives and with the Senate when it is under the control of the other party. As one who has been a Member of both bodies, I understand and I respect differences of opinion in both foreign and domestic policy . . . But I also know . . . that when the security of America is involved, when peace for America and for the world is involved . . . we are not Democrats, we are not Republicans, we are Americans.

Remarks in the House Chamber
November 13, 1969

"In the spirit of American football at its best, let's always try to be number one, because we owe it to ourselves, we owe it to our country. Second, in the spirit of American football, let's be for our team, let's be for our country. And as we look at this country, when we hear people say America is an ugly country, let's stand up and answer. Let's say this is a beautiful country and the glory of it is that we have the great opportunity to make it even more beautiful in the years to come."

Remarks at the
Professional Football Hall of Fame
Canton, Ohio
July 30, 1971

INTO THE SECOND TERM:

"Let us make the next four years the best fo

ars in America's history"

"I would only hope that in these next four years we can so conduct ourselves in this country, and so meet our responsibilities in the world in building peace in the world, that years from now people will look back to the generation of the 1970's, at how we have conducted ourselves, and they will say, 'God bless America.' "

Election night statement
November 7, 1972

From its very beginning, 1972 was a political year—one of the most hotly political in memory; but for President Nixon it had greater significance as a time of fruition when a whole range of patiently cultivated efforts toward peace abroad and reform at home would begin to mature. Nineteen seventy-one had seen announcements of the forthcoming summit meetings in Peking and in Moscow, a quickening of the secret quest for a Vietnam peace settlement, initiation of a New Economic Policy aimed at making '72 the "very good year" economically which the President had forecast, and steady progress in other areas of domestic affairs.

These concerns were the center of attention at the White House in the first days of January, 1972, when the President declared his intentions for the coming election in a brief letter to his chief political backer in New Hampshire, scene of the Nation's first Presidential primary two months hence.

"We have made significant beginnings in the past three years," the President wrote. "I want to complete the work that we have begun, and therefore I shall be a candidate for renomination and re-election. . . . (It is) my hope that together we can work toward a national renewal that will make the anniversary year of 1976 as proud a milestone for America as was 1776."

Throughout the year, even after the national party conventions and into the fall campaign, it was his duties as President rather than his ambitions as candidate that absorbed most of Richard Nixon's time and energies—to a degree which many observers thought remarkable. During a fast transcontinental campaign swing in late September, the President explained his thinking this way: "There is nothing I welcome more than the opportunity to take the case for this Administration, for the last 4 years and for the next 4 years, to the American people. But I believe my first obligation is to do my job as President of the United States of America. That is the reason why, when-

ever . . . I feel it is necessary to stay in Washington to do the job that the people elected me to do, I will be there. When I can, I will be campaigning."

Even so, between his virtually unanimous renomination at the Republican National Convention in Miami on August 22 and the election on November 7, the President campaigned in 19 States, and he reached millions of additional voters with a series of 14 nationwide radio speeches and a national television address comprehensively spelling out his positions on the issues.

His campaign statements evoked the Spirit of '76 again and again, urging the people to unite in a "New American Majority" transcending party labels, class, race, sections, and national origins, "so that we can make the next four years the best four years in America's history."

On election day, more than 46 million popular votes were cast for the Nixon-Agnew ticket, amounting to some 61 percent of the total and placing a record 49 States with 521 electoral votes in the President's column. When the almost un-

precedented proportions of his sweep became clear, President Nixon termed the landslide not so much a personal triumph as a potential "victory for America." It would be confirmed as a victory for America, he said, if the Nation moved forward from that day as one people committed to achieving those great goals which unite us above all partisanship or political differences.

Leading the country forward in that spirit has been the President's principal effort from November 8, 1972, up to the eve of his second inauguration on January 20, 1973—whether at the White House or at his retreats in Camp David and Key Biscayne where the pace of work only seems to intensify. He has taken vigorous and innovative steps to revitalize his Administration for the new term ahead, laid plans for constructive partnership with a new Congress still under opposition control, and pressed the search for peace. Plainly, as the United States moves into the homestretch toward its Bicentennial year, that essential spark of leadership at the top which Hamilton called "energy in the Executive" continues to characterize the Nixon Presidency.

FROM THE PRESIDENT'S ACCEPTANCE SPEECH TO THE REPUBLICAN NATIONAL CONVENTION AT MIAMI BEACH, AUGUST 23, 1972:

"I congratulate the delegates to this convention for renominating as my running-mate . . . Vice President Ted Agnew. I thought he was the best man for the job 4 years ago. I think he is the best man for the job today."

※

"I express my deep gratitude to this convention for the tribute that you have paid to the best campaigner in the Nixon family, my wife, Pat. In honoring her, you have honored millions of women in America who contributed in the past and will contribute in the future so very much to better government in this country."

※

"I pledge to you, all of the new voters in America who are listening here in this convention hall, that I will do everything that I can over these next four years to make your support be one that you can be proud of, because . . . years from now I want you to look back and be able to say that your first vote was one of the best votes you ever cast in your life."

"I ask you, my fellow Americans, tonight to join us, not in a coalition held together only by a desire to gain power. I ask you to join us as members of a new American majority bound together by our common ideals. I ask everyone listening to me tonight—Democrats, Republicans, Independents, to join our new majority— not on the basis of the party label you wear in your lapel, but on the basis of what you believe in your hearts."

※

"The choice in this election is not between radical change and no change. The choice in this election is between change that works and change that won't work."

※

"The chance America now has to lead the way to a lasting peace in the world may never come again. With faith in God and faith in ourselves and faith in our country, let us build a peace that our children and all the children of the world can enjoy for generations to come."

"Let me say that every one of us is proud
of his national background, but I say
that instead of referring to someone, 'He
is an Italian,' 'He is a German,' 'He is
a Pole,' 'He is a Ukranian,' let's say,
first of all, 'He or she is an American,'
because those who came to this shore . . .
have contributed so much to America. . . .
They believed in hard work. They didn't
come here for a handout. They came
here for an opportunity, and they built
America."

Remarks on Liberty Island, New York Harbor
September 26, 1972

"Tonight I would like to talk to you in
terms of not 'Democrats for Nixon,'
which puts it in highly personal terms,
but I would like to talk to you in terms
of 'Democrats for America,' which really
puts it where it belongs."

Remarks to a
gathering of Democrats at the
Connally Ranch, Floresville, Texas
September 22, 1972

"Tomorrow, 100 million Americans will have an opportunity to participate in a decision that will affect the future of America and the future of the world for generations to come. . . . You know what the issues are. You know that this is a choice which is probably the clearest choice between the candidates for President ever presented to the American people in this century. . . . I want to thank you for the honor of serving as President for the past 4 years, and regardless of your decision tomorrow, I can assure you that I shall continue to work for a goal that every American has: Let's make the next 4 years the best 4 years in America's history."

Remarks to the Nation on election eve
November 6, 1972

LOOK TO THE FUTURE was the title of the President's nationally televised address to the American people on November 2, 1972, in the closing days of the election campaign. In it he outlined his hopes for America in the years between now and 1976, saying in part:

"I want Americans—all Americans—to see more clearly and to feel more deeply what it is that makes this Nation of ours unique in history, unique in the world, a nation in which the soul and spirit are free, in which each person is respected, in which the individual human being, each precious, each different, can dare to dream and can live his dreams. . . .

"I want each American—all Americans—to find a new zest in the pursuit of excellence, in striving to do their best and to be their best, in learning the supreme satisfaction of setting a seemingly impossible goal, and meeting or surpassing that goal, of finding in themselves that extra reserve of energy or talent or creativity that they had not known was there. . . .

"When I think of what America means. . .I think of one person, one child—any child. That one child is America, with a life still ahead, with his eyes filled with dreams, and with the birthright of every American child to a full and equal opportunity to pursue those dreams."

In a radio speech three days later, the President elaborated on this idea of the birthright of an American child, outlining ten goals which he called "campaign promises which America should make to itself" regarding the kind of country in which the children of the Bicentennial Era will grow up. The goals were:

- An America at peace in a world at peace
- A more just America
- A healthy America
- A well-educated America
- A secure and prosperous America
- A liveable America
- An America free from fear
- A free and self-governed America
- A pluralist, open America
- A great and a good America

"Let all Americans . . . take them as our guides on election day and every day throughout the next 4 years," the President said of these ten points. "If we do this, then I believe that this election of 1972 will be remembered as one of America's finest hours, and that the next 4 years will be the best 4 years in America's first two centuries."

"My approach to the second term is that of a Disraeli conservative—a strong foreign policy, strong adherence to basic values that the Nation believes in and the people believe in, and to conserving those values, and not being destructive of them, but combined with reform, reform that will work, not reform that destroys . . .

"This election will demonstrate that the American people . . . will thrive upon a new feeling of responsibility, a new feeling of self-discipline . . . It is our responsibility to find a way to reform our government institutions so that this new spirit of independence, self-reliance, pride, that I sense in the American people can be nurtured."

Washington Star-News interview
November 9, 1972

"We feel that we have a mandate . . . to continue to provide change that will work in our foreign policy and in our domestic policy, change that will build a better life, that will mean progress at home toward our great goals here, just as we have been making progress in the field of international affairs."

Remarks to the press
November 27, 1972

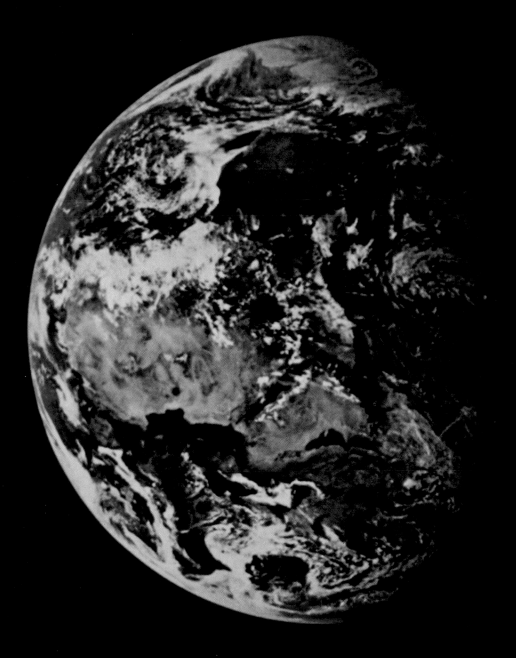

'. . . *our destiny lies not in the stars but on earth itself, in our own hands, in our own hearts.*''

First Inaugural Address
January 20, 1969

THE VICE PRESIDENT

"...a man of courage and conviction"

"Perhaps it is the man himself who makes or breaks the Vice Presidency. Certainly in the case of Ted Agnew there can be no doubt that he has made this office one of the most significant platforms for moral and political leadership in our nation."

President Nixon
May 19, 1972

Richard Nixon, who has a deep and a personal understanding of the Vice Presidency, has described Vice President Agnew's accomplishments in office this way:

"Perhaps it is the man himself who makes or breaks the Vice Presidency. Certainly, in the case of Ted Agnew there can be no doubt that he has made this office one of the most significant platforms for moral and political leadership in our Nation.

"At a time when so many are calling for candor from our public officials, we can point with pride to the man who was speaking out long before it became fashionable. Here is a man of courage and conviction. The respect we share for him stems as much from our understanding of his devotion to creating a better America, as it does from our appreciation of his candor and boldness in speaking out for what he believes is right.

". . . He has shown by his firmness and fortitude that he is truly a representative of the spirit that has made and will keep our Nation great."

As the President so eloquently pointed out, the Vice President is known to millions of Americans for his candor—his willingness to speak out, to call things as he sees them, even when it is not politically expedient or popular to do so. He is also widely known, through his public speeches, for his demonstrated belief in and his concern for the basic, fundamental principles of truth and patriotism and justice that have made America a great Nation.

Perhaps less known, however, are his day to day executive responsibilities as Vice President, a role that has been broadened by President Nixon. The Vice President has recognized his responsibility as a team player whose role it is to carry out those tasks assigned him by the President.

Of primary importance in the past four years has been the key role he has performed as the President's liaison with the Governors, Mayors, and County officials of this country in an effort to implement the President's policy of restoring State and local government to equal partnership in the Federal system.

As a former County Executive and Governor, the Vice President has brought to this role a first-hand knowledge of the difficulties and frustrations so often brought about by the Federal Government's lack of understanding of the particular needs and desires of State and local elected officials. He has worked to sensitize the Federal Government to those needs. And he has succeeded.

Perhaps the most conspicuous success has been his leadership in marshaling State and local support for passage of Revenue Sharing. The Vice

"*A President lives in the spotlight, but a Vice President lives in the flickering strobe lights that alternately illuminate or shadow his unwritten duties. It is sometimes uncomfortable. It is sometimes ego-diminishing. But it is also quietly rewarding—this Office of the Vice Presidency—particularly rewarding if you serve with a great President, as has been my good fortune.*"

Vice President Agnew's acceptance speech
Republican National Convention, 1972

President kept this effort alive at a time when knowing pundits and many Congressional leaders had declared it dead. It was largely due to his efforts that Revenue Sharing did not collapse into the grave its opponents had dug for it. And day in and day out, in a quiet, business-like manner, he has worked to assure that the views and suggestions of State and local officials on domestic problems were made an integral part of Federal decision making.

Such Federal programs as general and special Revenue Sharing, foster care, manpower training, the summer youth program, wage and price controls, and many others bear the imprint of the Vice President's advice and action on behalf of State and local governments and the millions of people they represent.

Recent statements by two of the Nation's leading local officials attest to the success the Vice President has achieved in this role. John Gunther, Executive Director of the U. S. Conference of Mayors, said: "Federal-City relations over the past two and one-half years have been the best I have seen since coming to Washington in 1946. The Vice President, through the Office of Intergovernmental Relations, has been of immeasurable assistance to the Nation's cities."

And Bernard Hillenbrand, Executive Director of the National Association of Counties, in a recent telegram to the President, said: "One of the most outstanding successes of the Nixon Administration has been the establishment of the Office of Intergovernmental Relations under the direct supervision of the Vice President. This office has proved to be the ombudsman for States, counties and cities in wading through the Federal bureaucratic red tape. The National Association of Counties wants to congratulate you, Mr. President, for your foresight and the Vice President for a job well done."

In other little-publicized areas, the Vice President's accomplishments have been equally impressive. As Chairman of the National Council on Indian Opportunity, he was the key mover in the formulation of the President's Indian policy, which is recognized as the most progressive ever undertaken to solve the problems of the American Indian. He was also a major force in the President's successful efforts to redress long-time grievances by returning sacred lands to the Taos Pueblo Indians of New Mexico and the Yakima Indians of Washington and in the historic settlement of Alaskan native claims.

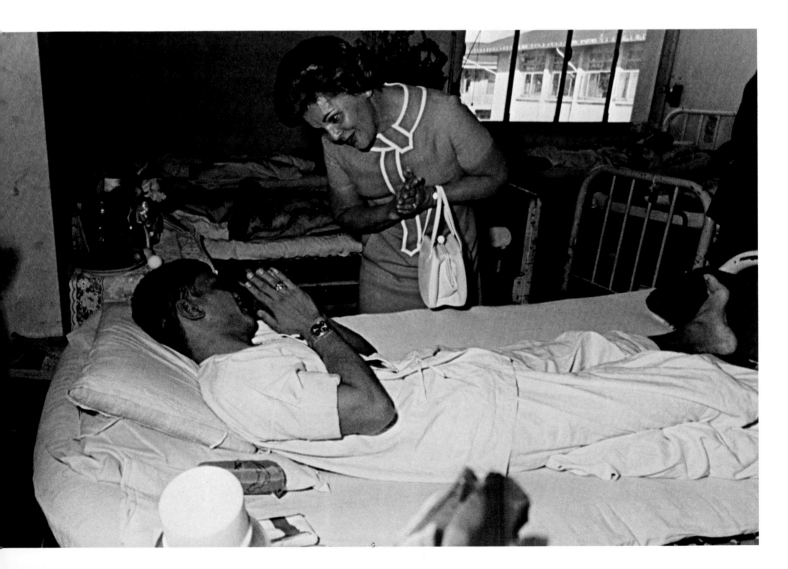

"No matter is of more central concern to this nation today than the proper growth and development of our young people. . . . Our young people are, in the most basic sense, our greatest national resource, and our future as a nation depends upon how well we treasure and nurture that resource."

Vice President Agnew
September 20, 1972

The Vice President has also carried out with distinction his assignment as Chairman of the National Aeronautics and Space Council. He has been one of the most consistent and eloquent champions of America's role in space, and he has played an active role in developing the comprehensive programs of space activities conducted by various Federal departments and agencies. In this capacity, he has also insured effective cooperation among these departments and agencies, and, when necessary, has played an active role in resolving differences and setting priorities. Under the Vice President's direction, this council periodically surveyed significant space-related activities in the private sector.

The Vice President has been actively involved in the conduct of foreign affairs. He is a member of the National Security Council, and when the President is absent, acts as its Chairman. As a result, he has played an important role in this Administration in the formulation of foreign policy.

In addition to having met with most of the ambassadors in Washington and with the heads of state and other high-ranking officials from more than 40 countries during the course of their visits to this country, the Vice President is an experienced emissary. In five official foreign visits since taking office, he has spent over 80 days abroad.

These missions, on behalf of the President, have taken him to 28 different countries. In each he has met with top leadership and a widely representative group of citizens. Thus, on the basis of first-hand knowledge, the Vice President has been able to provide timely reports and advice for the President on a broad spectrum of foreign policy issues involving some of the most critical areas of the world as well as relations with some of our closest allies. He has visited the Republic of Vietnam on three occasions.

In his travels, the Vice President has talked at length with many able and renowned leaders throughout the world. He is well-acquainted personally with almost every leader in Southeast Asia, and in his meetings with them he has served as a much needed high-level point of contact—both in explaining U.S. policies, and giving encouragement and support to our allies.

And finally, of course, there are the outstanding accomplishments of the Vice President as a spokesman and campaigner for his party. During the campaign of 1970, Vice President Agnew visited 40 cities in 30 States, logging 35,394 total air miles on behalf of Congressional, Senatorial and State and local candidates. And in the campaign of 1972, he was his party's chief campaigner, traveling 43,972 air miles to speak for State and national

candidates and for the re-election of the President in 56 cities in 36 States.

Vice President Agnew has brought new dignity and scope to the office of the Vice Presidency, an often controversial office whose function was perhaps best described by the Vice President himself in accepting nomination for a second term at Miami Beach last August.

"Surely, much of the controversy about the Vice Presidency could be quieted," he said, "if we would accept the fact that the Vice President is the President's man and not a competing political entity. He accepts the investiture of Presidential trust, runs on the same platform, and must be a man upon whom the President can depend for total loyalty and support.

"He is a part of the President's team, contributing candidly his best advice in the formulation of policies and, once these policies are formulated, helping translate them into achievements. That is the way I view the office and I believe that is the true spirit and meaning of the 12th amendment, which for 168 years has required that the President and Vice President run together and be elected as a team."

A comprehensive definition, and one that sums up admirably the role that Vice President Agnew has played in this Administration.

". . . He has shown by his firmness and fortitude that he is truly a representative of the spirit that has made and will keep our nation great."

President Nixon
May 19, 1972

THE *Pat* NIXON YEARS

... Partner to a President

"Being First Lady has given me
an opportunity to meet people
around the world and share
their hopes and dreams . . . also
to undertake projects which
will contribute to the quality
of life for everyone."

The members of the United States Congress, assembled in joint session for a Presidential report on the Moscow summit, came to their feet with waves of enthusiastic applause for her winning way with the Russian and Chinese peoples when she entered to take her seat in the gallery.

The President said of her precedent-making diplomatic mission to West Africa on his behalf, "I realized that the substitute was doing a much better job than the principal would have done."

She "unquestionably has knocked herself out the past four years," a Washington reporter says, "playing gracious hostess to hordes of visitors."

Accepting renomination at the Republican National Convention in August, 1972, her husband saluted her as "the best campaigner in the Nixon family."

Decorators and historic preservation experts acclaimed her refurbishing of the state rooms of the White House as having brought to the Executive Mansion the most distinguished art and authentic furniture in its 172-year history.

And one of her daughters confides that in the growing-up years, "Daddy was sort of a soft touch, but we knew that Mother would lay down the law to us."

"The trips to China and Russia have been the high points of my first four years in the White House because these were journeys for peace . . . and I believe we will eventually achieve the peace my husband has been seeking for so long."

She is Patricia Ryan Nixon, wife of the President, 35th First Lady of the United States, known and loved by millions of people in this country and around the world as "Pat." A quarter of a century in public life with her husband and four years as hostess at the White House haven't really changed her, she says; it's just that "now people have a chance to know what the real Pat Nixon is like."

The real Pat Nixon is, among other things, the most widely traveled First Lady in history. Since 1953, Mrs. Nixon has visited 75 countries. Everywhere she has gone, her natural warmth, her sincere interest in people, and her unique ability to make friends have advanced the cause of human understanding.

As First Lady, Mrs. Nixon accompanied the President on his round-the-world trip in 1969 and on his mission to Europe in 1970, her intensive personal schedule in each country taking her out to meet people of all ages and all walks of life.

In May, 1970, she flew to Peru following the devastating earthquake to focus world attention on the plight of the victims and to launch a volunteer American relief drive in their behalf. She toured the quake-shattered Andean villages, bringing not only moral support but also clothing, food and other supplies donated by the people of the United States. The Peruvian Government selected her as the first North American woman to receive its highest honor—the Grand Cross of the Order of the Sun.

"*I've been traveling on the international scene since 1953, and I did all the things I do today. But, of course, our trips then were not covered so well by the media. Now people have a chance to know what the real Pat Nixon is like.*"

FOREIGN COUNTRIES VISITED BY MRS. NIXON AS FIRST LADY

1969	Philippines	1970	Peru	1972	Liberia
	Indonesia		Mexico		Ghana
	Vietnam		Italy		Ivory Coast
	Thailand		Yugoslavia		People's Republic of China
	Pakistan		Spain		Canada
	Romania		Great Britain		Austria
	Great Britain		Ireland		U.S.S.R.
					Iran
					Poland

In January, 1972, Mrs. Nixon undertook a nine-day mission of personal diplomacy to West Africa which heightened her credentials as an ambassador of American goodwill. The President, unable to accept an invitation to the inauguration of Liberian President William Tolbert, designated the First Lady as his official representative for the occasion. It was the first such mission ever undertaken by the wife of an American President, and the first visit ever paid by a President or his lady to Ghana, Ivory Coast, and Liberia. Affectionate crowds met her in each country, and she came home to glowing national praise.

Later in 1972, Pat Nixon played a key role in the President's trip to the People's Republic of China and then in his historic state visit to the Soviet Union.

On both of these trips, President Nixon's time was largely absorbed with conferences and nego-tiations, so it fell to his wife to carry the spirit of American friendship into the schools, hospitals, work places, and street scenes closer to the every-day lives of the people of these long-time adver-saries of the United States. This she did with spirit and success.

She calls these two trips the high point of her first four years as First Lady. "These were jour-neys for peace," she says, "and I believe we will eventually achieve the peace my husband has been seeking for so long."

At home, Mrs. Nixon has concentrated over the past four years on "bringing the White House to the people."

She has worked to give new impetus to volun-teerism—the traditional American spirit of helping others in need—by visiting volunteer projects throughout the country, by inviting outstanding volunteers to the White House, and by writing

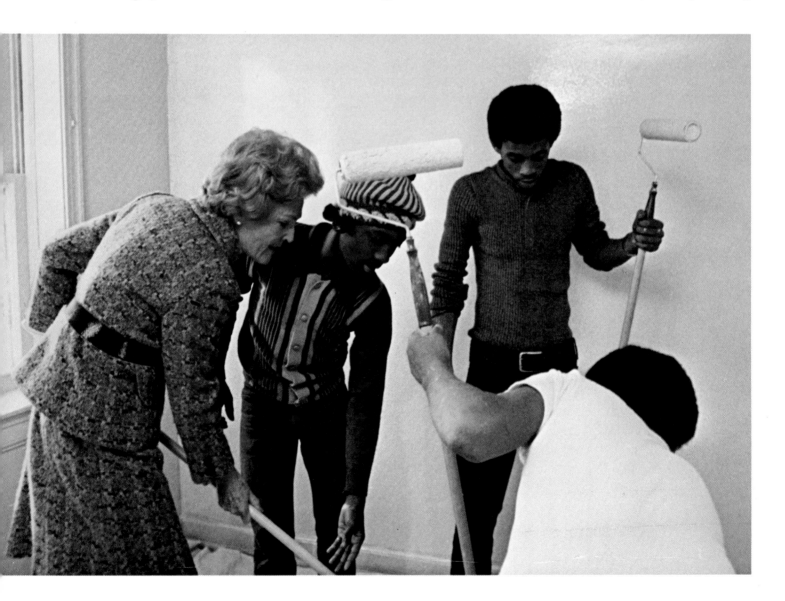

personal letters of commendation.

Another concern which has taken the First Lady from coast to coast is President Nixon's drive to bring America's parklands closer to the people. In August, 1971, she visited Virginia, Michigan, Minnesota, Oregon, and California on a three-day tour in the interest of the Administration's "Legacy of Parks" program, under which Federal lands are turned over to States and communities for park and recreational use. In ceremonies along the way, Mrs. Nixon officiated at the transfer of a total of more than 4,000 acres of real estate worth some $11 million. She has maintained her interest in this program since then, as have her daughters, Julie Eisenhower and Tricia Cox, both of whom have represented the President at Legacy of Parks ceremonies in a number of States.

Because both the President and Mrs. Nixon firmly believe that the White House "belongs to

"Although volunteerism has been a sustaining principle throughout our Nation's history, the need for personal concern and involvement in today's complex world is more vital than ever. Our success as a Nation depends upon our willingness to give generously of ourselves for the welfare and enrichment of the lives of others."

"Dick and I have felt a strong responsibility for preserving the White House in all its historic beauty for the American people. We have tried to open the doors of this house to people from all walks of life, both in this country and abroad."

the American people," she has worked to make this rich historical heritage more meaningful to every visitor.

This has meant personally involving herself in a complete renovation of the state rooms of the historic mansion, planning its exterior illumination at night, expanding White House tours for the physically handicapped, and putting on display for the public state gifts and historic objects formerly kept in private family quarters.

Her idea for the nocturnal illumination of the White House was born on the evening of Inauguration Day, 1969. As Mrs. Nixon recalls it: "That evening when we had been to all of the balls and came back, all the members of the family stood around reliving the excitement. I asked Dick to turn on all of the lights in the White House, which he did, and there was a blaze of light for all to see."

Thereafter, Mrs. Nixon spent months studying diagrams of the White House and its grounds, and with the help of experts and using funds from the 1969 inauguration, she helped plan the Mansion's exterior illumination, which was completed in November, 1970.

The First Lady then turned her attention to the interior of the Mansion. Since its last renovation in 1961, ten years and millions of visitors had taken their toll, and Mrs. Nixon decided that a major refurbishing was necessary.

So that the White House would not be closed to regular visitors, she chose to work on one room at a time. Since the Congress makes no appropriations of funds for White House refurbishing or acquisitions, Mrs. Nixon had to raise funds and gather acquisitions from private sources.

She personally helped to acquire many objects and pieces of furniture of historic interest for the restoration. She was able, for example, to arrange for the return of Gilbert Stuart's famous portrait of Dolley Madison to hang in the redecorated Red Room on loan from the Pennsylvania Academy of the Fine Arts. The painting had hung there originally when it was Mrs. Madison's sitting room, but had not been back to the White House since it was removed when the British burned Washington in 1814. Mrs. Nixon has also taken the lead in greatly expanding the White House collection of portraits of the First Ladies to complement the Mansion's fine display of paintings of the Presidents.

Not long after the widely acclaimed refurbishment project was officially completed with the reopening of the Blue Room to the public in May, 1972, Mrs. Nixon took off her decorator's cap and put on yet another of the many hats she has worn with flair as First Lady—this one the straw boater of an energetic and winsome campaign emissary to that "New American Majority" which the President sought to assemble in his 1972 re-election effort.

While her husband was able to undertake only a

light schedule of political travel during the summer and fall because of the demands of his job, Mrs. Nixon spent many days on the hustings in his behalf, covering more than 22,000 miles and visiting 16 States between the Republican Convention and the election. With a similar zest for reaching out to the people, Tricia Cox also campaigned in 16 States, logging more than 33,000 miles, while Julie Eisenhower's campaign odyssey totaled 38,000 miles across 23 States.

With "four more years" now ahead, the First Lady plans to continue pursuing all of her special duties and projects into the President's second term. These will include her volunteer projects, the constant concern for the living White House, the special tours for the handicapped, active personal involvement in answering her own mail from all over the world, and the myriad other challenging duties of being a President's lady and official hostess at the White House.

Pat Nixon's greatest sense of personal fulfillment comes, she says, "in being a partner to a great man —the greatest experience one could possibly have." In that experience she feels that she has come to know the spirit of America—its hopes and dreams, its compassion and understanding, its courage and noble ambition to serve all mankind.

As Mrs. Nixon has traveled the country, she has seen this spirit, the Spirit of '76, in hundreds of varied settings—in a State fair in Oklahoma, in a centennial celebration, in the faces of volunteers working in the inner city. She sums up her reaction in a few words: "I am so heartened to see that the spirit of America is still strong."

"I don't think you ever think of it quite as 'home.' Still it is very fascinating to live here and with our close family ties, our daughters have been able to share this experience with us and also make their contribution . . . I really have enjoyed being here and being able to support many programs in which I believe."

J. Willard Marriott, CHAIRMAN

HONORARY CHAIRMEN
Mrs. Tobin Armstrong
Elmer Bobst
Jesse Calhoon
Robert S. Carter
Francis Dale
Thomas B. Evans, Jr.
William Lucy
Mrs. J. Willard Marriott
Hon. John A. Nevius
Edmund Pendleton, Jr.
Hon. James Roosevelt
Hon. Walter Washington

OFFICE OF THE CHAIRMAN
William J. McManus, Special Advisor
S. Dillon Ripley, Special Advisor
Warren K. Hendriks, Jr., Executive Assistant
Mervel Denton, Executive Secretary
Robert W. Barker, General Counsel
Glenn J. Sedam, Jr., Deputy General Counsel
Herbert E. Marks, Associate General Counsel
Pierre J. LaForce, Associate General Counsel
Joseph J. Adams, Associate General Counsel
Joseph W. Barr, Treasurer
L. A. Jennings, Guarantee Fund
G. Dewey Arnold,
   Chairman, Insurance Committee
Ann L. Dore, Press Aide
Major Kenneth H. Nash, USA, Military Aide

VICE CHAIRMEN
Mrs. Norman C. Armitage
Kenneth M. Crosby
Hon. Robert Dole
Mark Evans
Frank Fitzsimmons
Daniel T. Kingsley
Hobart Lewis
Major Gen. C. S. O'Malley, Jr
   USA (Ret.)
Leonard M. Marks
H. Ross Perot
Mrs. Donald Rumsfeld
Samuel Schulman
C. Robert Yeager
J. Hillman Zahn

Jeb S. Magruder, EXECUTIVE DIRECTOR

OFFICE OF THE EXECUTIVE DIRECTOR
Mrs. Claire L. Chennault, Special Advisor
Herbert L. Porter, Assistant Executive Director
Charles J. Reisler, III, Administrative Assistant
James L. Kolstad, Director, Invitation Control
Anthony J. McDonald, Jr.,
   Director, Advertising and Promotion

Thomas A. Slivinski,
   Director, Program Planning
Powell A. Moore, Director, Press Relations
Arthur Amolsch,
   Deputy Director, Press Relations
Frederick L. Webber, Congressional Liason

1973 INAUGURAL ADVISORY COMMITTEE

Hon. Nathan G. Agostinelli
Mrs. Harlan J. Anderson
Mr. Clarence Arata
Mr. Frank Barnett
Mr. Ralph Becker
Mrs. Fitzgerald Bemiss
Mr. R. Burdell Bixby
Mr. Tom Bolger
Mr. James H. Boyce
Mr. Jesse Brent
Mr. Raymond L. Brown
Hon. William A. Burden
Mr. William R. Campbell, Jr.
Mr. William S. Campbell
Mr. William P. Clements, Jr.
Mr. George Champion
Mr. Albert Cole
Hon. John F. Collins
Mr. Marvin Collins
Mr. Richard J. (Boone) Comer
Mr. George Cook
Mr. Howard V. Corcoran
Mrs. Patricia Nixon Cox
Mrs. Joe Crossan
Mr. Thomas G. Crouch
Hon. G. W. Deschamps
Mr. Fred Dixon
Hon. Donald Dwight

Hon. Lane Dwinell
Mrs. Julie Nixon Eisenhower
Hon. James S. Erwin
Mr. Robert Flanigan
Mr. Ed Foley
Mr. Peter Fosco
Mr. G. Robert Gadberry
Mr. John A. (Jack) Gibbs
Mr. Jack Gibson
Mr. Thomas Gleason
Mr. Gordon Gooch
Mr. Pat Gorman
Mrs. Robert Gosman
Mr. C. Eugene Goss
Mr. Paul Govora
Mr. Raymond E. Guest
Mr. Paul Hall
Mr. Ed Hartman
Hon. Will H. Hays, Jr.
Mr. James M. Henderson
Mr. Ed Hoffman
Mr. Thomas Houser
Mr. Charles Jonas, Jr.
Mr. John Kauffman
Mr. Allan G. Kaupinen
Hon. David Kennedy
Mr. George Killion
Mr. John Kluge

Mr. Willie Leftwich
Mr. Gustave Levy
Mr. Willard Lewis
Mr. Gordon Luce
Mrs. Russell T. Lund
Mr. Ken Lyons
Mr. Walter McArdle
Mr. Foster McGaw
Mr. W. I. McKnight
Mr. John K. MacIver
Mrs. Charles Malone
Hon. Sam Mardian
Mr. John B. Mason
Mr. Weldon Mathis
Mrs. Robert K. Michael
Mr. Raymond B. Milici
Mr. Dale Miller
Mr. Donald M. Mosiman
Mrs. Rex Moore
Mr. John W. Mooty
Mr. Richard D. Murray
Mr. Lyn Nofziger
Mr. Ed Nixon
Mr. George Nowotny
Mr. W. E. "Obie" O'Brien
Mr. John Olin
Mr. B. Waring Partridge
Mr. William H. Perkins, Jr.

Hon. Jack Ray
Mr. Clark Reed
Mr. Thomas C. Reed
Mr. Richard (Dick) Richards
Mr. Meshulan Riklis
Hon. Lawrence K. Roos
Mr. Charles D. Ross
Mr. John Rouzie
Mr. Peter R. Sawers
Mr. Richard Scaife
Hon. Harry L. Sears
Mrs. Elmer M. Smith
Hon. Arlen Specter
Hon. John D. Spellman
Mr. John Stadler
Mr. Ned Sullivan
Hon. James L. Taft, Jr.
Hon. Edward P. Thomas
Mr. L. E. (Tommy) Thomas
Mr. Reid Thompson
Mr. Charles Van Horn
Mr. Graham Watt
Mr. Hunter P. Wharton
Mr. Churchill Williams
Hon. Wendall Wyatt
Dr. Clayton K. Yeutter
Hon. Clifford Young

GROUP I

Daniel T. Kingsley, Vice Chairman
John E. Clarke, Group Director
Finance Committee
    Dan Searby, Chairman
    Leo Nielson, Co-Chairman
    James Councilor, Comptroller
    Bud Murray, Budget Manager
    Joseph Lynn, Accounting Manager
Personnel
    Sam Schulhof, Chairman
Records Control Committee
    Jerry Wallace, Chairman
Information Center
    Biba Wagner, Chairman
Facilities and Equipment Committee
    Ted Garrish, Chairman
    Mike Sterlacci, Director
Correspondence Committee
    Diane Weir, Chairman
Purchase and Procurement Committee
    Jerald Sternburg, Chairman
Transportation Committee
    James Arthur, Chairman
    Robert Bannon, Director
Volunteers Committee
    Sally Nevius, Chairman
    Mrs. Meg Keech,
        Co-Chairman Placement
    Mrs. Jan Evans,
        Co-Chairman Records
    Mrs. Jean Fangboner,
        Co-Chairman Records
    Mrs. Sylvia Hermann,
        Co-Chairman Recruitment
    Mrs. Rosemary Foeman,
        Co-Chairman Recruitment
Invitation Support Committee
    Frank Wall, Chairman

GROUP II

Mark Evans, Vice Chairman
Kenneth Rietz, Group Director
Inaugural Balls Committee
    Kimball C. Firestone, Chairman
    Mrs. Vince Lombardi, Co-Chairman
    George Webster, Co-Chairman
    Tom Bell, Director
The Inaugural Concerts
    Pam Powell, Chairman
    Bart Starr, Co-Chairman
    Charlton Heston, Co-Chairman
    Ken Smith, Director
Symphonic Concert
    Rev. Billy Graham, Chairman
    William H. G. FitzGerald, Co-Chairman
    W. Clement Stone, Co-Chairman

American Music Concert
    Nat Winston, Chairman
    Floyd McKissick, Co-Chairman
    Mary Ann Mobley, Co-Chairman
Youth Concert
    Mike Curb, Chairman
    Jody Smith, Co-Chairman
    Joann Cullen, Co-Chairman
Candlelight Dinners Committee
    Bernard J. Lasker, Chairman
    George B. Cook, Co-Chairman
    John W. Rollins, Co-Chairman
    Nancy Harvey Steorts, Director
Vice President's Reception
    The Hon. Helen Delich Bentley, Chairman
    Bernard J. Lasker, Chairman
    Charles Bresler, Director
Salute to the States
    Bob Hope, Entertainment Chairman
        and Master of Ceremonies
    Thomas S. Markey, Chairman
    Mrs. Nelson A. Rockefeller, Chairman
    Terry Ann Meeuwsen, Co-Chairman
    Max M. Fisher, Co-Chairman
    Ben Cotten, Director
Entertainment
    Bob Hope, Chairman
    Frank Sinatra, Chairman
    Sammy Davis, Jr., Chairman
    Ray Caldiero, Director
    Ed Cowling, Deputy Director
Tickets
    Ruth Packard, Chairman
    Barbara Higgins, Director

GROUP III

J. Hillman Zahn, Vice Chairman
Michael Raoul-Duval, Group Director
Licenses & Concessions
    J. E. Reinke, Chairman
    Mark Sandground, Co-Chairman
    Dr. Ed G. Smith, Jr., Co-Chairman
    John S. Guthrie, Director
Marketing and Distribution
    Leonidas T. Delyannis, Chairman
    Julian Gillespie, Co-Chairman
    Richard Tribbe, Co-Chairman
    Alan M. Pottasch, Director
Medals and Program Book
    J. Paull Marshall, Chairman
    Dr. Darrell Crain, Co-Chairman
    Paul O'Brien, Co-Chairman
    Allen Hall, Director
Parade
    Robert Collier, Chairman
    George Allen, Co-Chairman
    John Morrissey, Co-Chairman
    Jon A. Foust, Director

1973 INAUGURAL STAFF (Con't.)

GROUP IV

Kenneth M. Crosby, Vice Chairman
Webster B. Todd, Jr., Group Director

Youth Inaugural Committee
    Don Sundquist, Chairman
    Joe Abate, Co-Chairman
    Gary Hughes, Co-Chairman
    Angie Miller, Co-Chairman
    George Gorton, Director

State Societies
    Lawrence Temple, Chairman
    Mrs. Darrell Trent, Co-Chairman
    Frank Tufaro, Co-Chairman
    William Minshall, III, Director

Religious Host Groups
    Arthur Flemming, Chairman
    Wendell G. Eames, Co-Chairman
    Dr. Edward L. R. Elson, Co-Chairman
    Roger Stone, Director

Veterans
    Gen. Omar Bradley, Chairman
    Adm. Arleigh Burke, Chairman
    Col. Frank Borman, Chairman
    Gjore Mollenhoff, Director

Governor's Host Committee
    Hon. Linwood Holton, Chairman
    Hon. Jack Williams, Chairman
    Eleanor Williams, Co-Chairman and Director

Special Groups
    Tom Pappas, Chairman
    Dr. Manuel Giberga, Co-Chairman
    Phil Guarino, Co-Chairman
    Berkeley Burrell, Co-Chairman
    Irene Walczak, Co-Chairman
    Benjamin Fernandez, Co-Chairman
    Father Martin J. McManus, Co-Chairman
    John L. Wilks, Director

GROUP V

Mrs. Donald Rumsfeld, Vice Chairman
J. Curtis Herge, Group Director

Civic Participation
    Don Bittinger, Chairman
    Tedson Meyers, Co-Chairman
    Walter Johnson, Co-Chairman
    Paul Christian, Director

Hospitality
    Mrs. Robert Steeves, Chairman
    Harold Fangboner, Chairman
    Mrs. Harold Fangboner, Co-Chairman
    Harold F. Greene, Co-Chairman
    Mrs. Randolph Frank, Co-Chairman
    Richard Haase, Co-Chairman
    Barry Wright, Co-Chairman
    Mrs. Bertrand Adkins, Co-Chairman
    Susan Davis, Director

Housing
    Austin Kenny, Co-Chairman
    Leonard Hickman, Co-Chairman
    William McConnell, Co-Chairman
    Martin Perper, Director

GROUP VI

General Charles S. O'Malley, Jr., Vice Chairman
Dewey Clower, Group Director
John Gartland, Assistant Group Director

Armed Forces Committee
    Major Gen. J. B. Adamson, USA, Chairman
    Brig. Gen. Tom Brown, Director

Public Service
    Chief Jerry Wilson, Chairman
    Lt. Joseph Mazur, Director

Medical Committee
    Milton Cobey, M.D., Chairman

Grandstand & Bleachers
    Col. Sam Starobin, USA (Ret.), Chairman

"The 1973 Inaugural Committee gratefully acknowledges the many individuals and corporations that have subscribed to the 1973 Inaugural Guaranty Fund. Although the Presidential Inaugural Committee is created by Federal Statute, it is financed on a private enterprise basis. Therefore, to the many people who have given the Inaugural Committee the support needed to begin work for this historic occasion, the Inaugural Committee extends its thanks."

1973 INAUGURAL BOOK PUBLICATION STAFF

MANAGING EDITOR: Leroy L. Preudhomme

PHOTO & RESEARCH EDITORS:
    William W. Parish, Georg Whitlock
RESEARCH ASSISTANT: Clarice Woodley

ART & PRODUCTION: Al Josephson, Donald Vendl
PRODUCTION COORDINATION:
    Thomas C. Jones, J. G. Ferguson Publishing Co.
PRINTING: Photopress, Inc.
BINDING: Engdahl Co.
TYPOGRAPHER: The Poole Clarinda Company-Div.
    of American Can Company

Credits and Acknowledgements

White House photographs
under supervision of Ollie Atkins,
personal photographer to President Richard Nixon.

SPIRIT OF '76 by A. M. Willard from the original now at Abbott Hall, Marblehead, Mass. Also known as "Yankee Doodle." The only exact copy presented by Russell W. Knight to Washington Crossing Foundation at Washington Crossing, Pa.